Turning PDCA into a Routine for Learning

Mohammed Hamed Ahmed Soliman

Published by personal-lean.org, 2020.

While every precaution has been taken in the preparation of this book, the publisher assumes no responsibility for errors or omissions, or for damages resulting from the use of the information contained herein.

TURNING PDCA INTO A ROUTINE FOR LEARNING

First edition. October 13, 2020.

ISBN: 9798863913780.

Written by Mohammed Hamed Ahmed Soliman.

Table of Contents

Turning PDCA into a Routine for Learning

. . . .

Mohammed Hamed Ahmed Soliman

Published by personal-lean.org, 2020.

While every precaution has been taken in the preparation of this book, the publisher assumes no responsibility for errors or omissions, or for damages resulting from the use of the information contained herein.

TURNING PDCA INTO A ROUTINE FOR LEARNING

First edition. October 13, 2020.

Dedication

I created this book with the help of many different business resources.

These academic articles and books are all cited at the end of this book. A number of people have influenced my learning journey and my entire career. I would like to acknowledge them here.

Esraa Soliman: My lovely wife and partner. She encouraged me to write and publish this work. In fact, she always encourages me to do creative

work.

Jeffrey Liker: Professor at the University of Michigan and author of *The Toyota Way* and the amazing Toyota series of books. His impressive work on Toyota inspired and influenced my learning about the Toyota Production System. I would really like to thank him for his indirect involvement

in this work. Many examples included in this book were originally from his books. Although I have never met Jeff face to face, we have had great communications over social media platforms.

Chris Duklet: A lean manufacturing leader from the United States who works in the field of healthcare. He has contributed to this work by reviewing the book prior to publication and giving me useful recommendations and advice.

Attia Gomaa: Professor at the American University in Cairo who influenced

my teaching career at the university and taught me how to become a good trainer.

Steven Borris: A business consultant, author, and friend from England who influenced my writing career. He encouraged me to write and publish. Steven was my mentor on lean manufacturing, helping me first to understand the basics, after which I developed my understanding through deep practice and self-directed learning.

Eslam Soliman: My friend and a professor at the Assiut University. His PhD is from the University of New Mexico. He has influenced my entire writing career by giving me recommendations and advice on how to write and publish. He revised my published works many times and kept inspiring me after every piece I wrote and published.

Plan-Do-check-Act-Cycle

Mistakenly, many people think plan-do-check-act (PDCA) is a continuous improvement cycle, even if they neglect the human part. PDCA does aim to improve the process, but if you have only improved the process without developing and teaching your people, you have put the process at risk of slipping back. People must be trained in the culture of continuous improvement so they can keep managing the process with the new method.

PDCA is actually a remarkable learning cycle because people learn by doing. The best thing is to pick up a real project and start improving a process (Soliman, 2016). You don't learn to play football by watching a game or golf by watching the coach. You have to practice under the watchful eye of the mentor to develop new habits and change the bad ones. An attentive coach is critical to helping you make a new method become routine.

Toyota has several steps in its problem-solving process, steps that cycle through the famous PDCA wheel (Liker, 2012):

1. Define the problem relative to the ideal (plan).
2. Grasp the current situation (plan).
3. Break down the problem into manageable pieces (plan).
4. Find the root cause of the problem (plan).
5. Develop countermeasures (plan).
6. Implement the solution (do).
7. Examine what the actual outcomes are (check).
8. Adapt, adjust, standardize and scale the solutions to other areas (act).

The plan phase is invoked five times before proceeding to the do phase. This is to ensure both the quality of the implementation and that the selected countermeasure will solve the problem. Lean emphasizes the plan. And the plan phase cannot be created without a daily observation at the gemba to find the root causes, gather facts, discuss things with the process operators and develop the best countermeasure from different alternatives.

Unfortunately, many leaders jump into the do phase without spending enough time observing the situation to find the real problem (Liker, 2015). The most enjoyable part for the leader is the "do," but jumping to the do usually results in a quick fix that not only might not solve the real problem, it could create wastes in other linked areas.

Jumping to the do phase can escalate the problem and make the solution very costly. Imagine the example of electrical problems in automobiles. In this case, the technician decided that the problem was in the spark plug coils pack. Changing that costs $350 dollar. Unfortunately, that wasn't the problem – a faulty engine control unit (ECU) was. Replacing the ECU cost $1,500. The waste in time, effort and resources led to a total cost of more than $1,850 (Soliman, 2014).

Define the problem relative to the ideal to find the current and ideal states. You might consider your quality ratio of 97 percent good, but any gap between the current state and what could be reached is an opportunity for your competitors. One of the main failures in this step is how people hide their problems because they fear blame. There is no culture of visualizing problems and surfacing issues. This always makes it difficult to define the problem and discover the gap between the current state and the ideal state.

Grasping the current situation is critical. Management decisions should be based on facts, not simply metrics or computerized reports. This is why it's so important for managers to go the gemba to see what reality is. Watch the process and look to solve the problem, and remember not to blame the people (Ahmed, 2014).

Break down the problem into manageable pieces. We have seen many companies set targets and cascade them down to the bottom levels. The leaders below are responsible for achieving this target in a timely manner. Top management may blame leaders if this target has not been achieved on time. Upper management also often sets too big of a target, such as an 80 percent improvement in quality improvement this year instead of 20 percent improvement for four years.

This is another example of poor management habits. Psychological experiments have proved that people tend to make progress on concrete, small goals rather than complex, large ones. Seeking large improvements at once will cause a system failure, especially when people are new to process improvement. Leaders have to be patient. Breaking down the target into small increments will encourage people to participate and act.

Finding the root cause of the problem. Remember that at first glance the problem can appear to be a person. But leaders have to dig deeper to find the true root cause. Overconfidence is one of the biggest barriers to problem-solving. Leaders think they know how to fix things and will follow the problem-solving process at a superficial level. Without the true root case, you probably will build a plan and invest in resources for something that is not going to work.

Select the suitable solution from different countermeasures that you have received from people involved in the process and from different perspectives. Lean encourages selecting a solution from different alternatives. Prioritize your options and select the countermeasure that has the highest chance of success. Perhaps you can choose one that is easier to try and relatively inexpensive. Then you have to develop your plan on who, when and where.

However, it is possible that spending time in the plan phase will not reveal the proper solution. At this point, a small pilot project might be necessary in an attempt to reveal the appropriate countermeasures.

Do: Only then can you go to the "do" phase and implement the countermeasures. Be careful, as many managers think that this phase is the end of the issue, and once they pushed the button the system will go live and run forever. Keeping the process monitored is necessary. Continue coaching and supporting people to avoid slipping back (Soliman, 2015).

You should also use metrics and post them in the workplace. This helps align people to common targets (Ahmed, 2013). Those metrics should be visualized in the workplace using visual boards. Later, the progress should be updated and discussed regularly. Use colors for in-progress targets and for the achieved targets. The metrics give a starting point to your workforce. What is our measurable target? Where are we? Where do we want to be?

In the "check" phase, remember that after implementing the solution, people will not always continue in the same way as you wished. They won't follow the standard all the time. Supporting people, continuously monitoring them, coaching them and developing them until the new way becomes a routine is the key to a perfect solution. You may not achieve this in the first PDCA cycle. So, you have to repeat it continuously and keep supporting people until the new standardized process becomes a routine.

The "act" phase is where the start of the next cycle begins. You next plan will be based on the feedback you received from the "check" stage. In this phase you, should figure out what did work, what didn't and standardize what worked.

PDCA and the New Routine for Learning

The key success of Toyota's continuous improvement process is the effort that managers or leaders put in people development through the PDCA cycle (Liker, 2012). It is a remarkable learning cycle. As you go through each PDCA, you will learn different and higher levels of skills. This should be done under the eye of the mentor. Practicing new behaviors will shift the employees out of their existing routine and, over time, influence people's thoughts and actions. In the long term, repeated new habits can lead to a culture of continuous improvement. People should follow plan-do-check-act so often that it becomes natural way of thinking.

If a problem crops up that you thought had been solved, the proper question would be have you rotated the PDCA wheels enough times? PDCA needs to spin a lot before you reach your target, achieve a stable process and form new habits.

The Plan Phase

Distinction between Management by Objectives and Lean management

Old management style focus on the results, while lean focus on the plan. The traditional management style can be seen in the management by objectives approach. While lean planning is based on a process known as "hoshin kanri."

MBO was first presented by Drucker (1954). MBO is considered a method of planning and control to achieve the quantitative results. The method is also called management by results MBR.

The approach involves setting some objectives along with an incentive program in order to achieve the business goals. Unfortunately, such an approach and the other management techniques are still being taught in many business schools neglecting the bad habits of the modern management and making the lean journey harder.

Indeed, there are many ways to achieve the quantitative targets without making real improvement. The MBO method may have worked in the earlier decades when the market condition was different. Now with the world events necessitating the reduction in wastes and maximizing the efficiency, the demand for real improvement has been increased.

For example, "10 percent cost reduction." Actually, there are many ways to reach this target, either by cutting some resources or improving the way of doing things. In the first option, you want to achieve a quick reduction and remain the same at what you are doing, in the second option you are searching for obviously perfection for longer-term financial benefit.

In MBO, since the objectives are focused on specific results the business needs, the top management sends this message to the down: "here is what we need and how your performance will be judged-go do your jobs and bring back the results whatever it takes." Metrics are used to measure the results, and control the employee rather than being a tool with the employee themselves to measure their own work progress. There are often some rewards for those who met the challenge. MBO ignores how the objectives are achieved as long as the results are got. What could make things harder are those bad managers who go aggressive in order to achieve the objectives putting pressure on people and pushing them to get quick results. And who failed to succeed may be downgraded position, punished, or left with no promotion. Some managers still have the sink or swim mentality. Those who find a way to succeed gets rewarded, others will let go.

Worse, the goals that have been set with MBO are magical goals that don't match the real state of the company. The senior managers who defined the goals have not been at the gemba before, so they are not aware of the real situation at the processes.

Gemba is the place where the value-creating work happens. It means go and see where the work is done to better understand the process and grasp the real situation. It also presents the Toyota way of developing their leaders. Toyota uses a parallel process called hoshin kanri for setting the targets and planning the achievement. Leaders, managers, and senior managers who have spent enough time at the gemba are contributed in the process of setting the company's goals. The company's vision, goals, and plans must be aligned for continuous improvement. Actually, the targets-setting process and the pursuit of targets cannot be independent, and it is far too focused on results without having a real understand of the means to get there. Also, before seeking for accomplishments and results, leaders should be developed patiently through a long training process to ensure that everyone has a deep understand about the process so he can turn those challenging objectives into an action plan to get stable results. The company's goals should be set and cascaded down to all levels to specific plans (means). A specific goal at the top management may have a different name at the operational level. For example, increasing the market share as a long-term vision specified at the top may require an increase of the quality at the down in the manufacturing process. Hoshin kanri is an open mind method. It looks for the innovative ways of achieving the goals and focuses on developing and coaching people on problems solving. Hoshin kanri is not just a management by both means and results. It also works under a self-development and a high motivated system.

Many companies are thinking that MBO as a tool is not a problem, but what is MBO as a tool? It is the managers making decisions about what they believe the business needs to go and turning those into objectives for their people. Sometimes objectives are being discussed among group of peoples, but often they are handed down from the top down. Since the focus is on the results only, there are many lost opportunities. MBO ignores the team orientation, the coaching process, the action plans, and the process of setting the goals which should be done by the leaders who know the real state of the company at all levels.

A good process of setting and planning the achievements will continually produce good results. A bad process might temporarily produce the results under the pressure of managers but things will slip back again. Actually, people should be respected and treated like partners in the business. They should believe in the power of the system and that they are doing this for their jobs to become easier. Also, if people are left to do the job without direct coaching and learning

to maintain sustainability and achieve stable results, they will not feel about the power of the system. Executives who want to get the results without any of this and they have failed and must start over to develop appropriate leader skills.

Some companies use a culture of blame upon failure, this drive people to hide problems and present only what is good. Also imagine an organization full of people blaming, complaining, justifying, defending, and building cases against others, when would the work get done?

Therefore, managers should manage the process not the results, act as facilitators not blamers, and pay attention to how the goals are achieved not just the metrics.

A few steps to be considered for a successful process of setting, aligning, and achieving the objectives during the **plan phase:**

✓ Establish a long-term reasonable vision based on what business needs and the current situation. Vision should be actionable, measurable, applicable, and have a time frame for achievement. It should match the current state of the company and the situation at the processes. However, some companies, and in crisis situations may find that using a long-term vision is useless. A 10-years vision wouldn't mean much if a company didn't exist in 12 months. So, targets should be set and adapted according to the real situation in order to help the company to survive and quickly bring the system to life.

✓ Senior managers, leaders at all levels, and those who have spent enough time at the gemba are those who should be involved in the process of setting the company's goals. They know how the work actually gets done and what opportunities for improvement available out there.

✓ Vision and goals should be shared with everyone in the organization, and cascaded down at all levels. Everyone must understand the goals and the intention behind them.

✓ Ensure people are trained enough to achieve the results appropriately. People should understand exactly what improvement is needed to achieve the results.

✓ At any organization, establishing a process like hoshin kanri or similar for setting and achieving the targets should be carried after the training and developing process to ensure that leaders are capable of taking challenge and managing the continuous improvement culture through the P-D-C-A cycle.

✓ Goals can be broken down into manageable pieces or few small targets in order to ensure the quality of implementation. It is good to slowly apply the

P-D-C-A cycle at every step taken toward the next target, and remove the obstacles as find. It is not favorable to apply a large improvement at once. If there are some obstacles there, the resistance would be huge and the process will fail. There is always an unclear territory that hides many obstacles; this would never be discovered unless we move forward to the next target and apply the continuous improvement cycle at every step taken.

✓ How are you managing to get there? This is the method of achieving the targets, it calls target means (plan). For each target the current condition should be specified as well as the target condition using the appropriated metric. In many conditions, setting a long-term plan for making improvement and try to follow it is like moving in a road full of fog, if goals are broken to small targets, they would become easier to manage. There should be a plan for reaching each target. The next plan will be set for the next target according to the progress and the accomplishments.

✓ Train leaders on problems solving. This is one of the most critical requirements to achieve the targets and remove the obstacles. Most of companies that fail to make real improvement and achieve good results have neglected the training and coaching as a necessary part of the process. Managers should dig deep in the details to discover root causes rather than jumping to solutions and the "do" phase in the continuous improvement cycle.

The Use of Incentives to Motivate Creative Thinking and Encourage Employees to Generate Ideas for the Plan

Taylor (1911) quoted "if each employee's compensation was linked to their output, their productivity would go up."

Normally, employees get paid to do their jobs. Salaries and other financial benefits are initially adapted to meet the employee satisfaction and the minimum expectation of the job role. Everyone will have a salary increase upon promoting position which depends on many things like proven of good leadership capability.

Lots of companies are using a reward system that is tied to specific metrics. Such a system can encourage individual behavior rather than a team orientation if not adapted properly. Everyone will strive to do the improvement for himself in the particular process he is managing to quickly get the results ignoring the overall performance of the plant and the real problem-solving process. There will be no permanent solution for the chronic problems as problems solving requires a team cooperation in order to set the countermeasures, remove the obstacles, and implement the plan.

For example, in a company, a 20% from the employees' monthly salary was cut and paid back to each one based on the accomplishments and the individual performance. The evaluation was being carried every 6 months and based on the measurable results outputted from each employee using some metrics. One of those targets for 2012 was to map certain processes and achieve numeric improvement in the value-added work for each process. One engineer from the working team commented to his leader: "frankly, we are going to get to you only what you need because this is how we get evaluated, but we can't guarantee the sustaining of this improvement unless the team members at the operation level are coached on how to properly do their job with the new way."

In Japan Toyota try to avoid tying specific rewards to specific metrics, fearing that employee would focus narrowly on what is measured and ignore the other parts of the job. Liker (2012) quoted "Psychological experiments show that paying people to do something that they already want to do either because they enjoy it or because they want to get good at it can kill the intrinsic motivation." The company will have to continually provide rewards if it wants to continue to see good behavior.

While Taylor focuses on individual incentives based on productivity, Toyota focus on team working and the evaluation is based on the group performance.

However, this is not to say that incentives should not be used at all. The incentives can still be based on team working, large accomplishments, and the plant performance. But it should not be tied to individual accomplishments.

Also, there are some morale motives that can reduce the demand of providing incentives such as: granting a certificate of appreciation to those who prove good things and good leadership capability, perform coaching and training and grant a certificate to those who pass the tests with remarkable results. Tests could be practical and real problem-solving ones. And if employees are practicing what they learn, their learning experience will be increased through the implementation. Both the organization and the employees are getting a benefit from the system now. Also, with coaching and certificating the successful, people will feel about the investment spent on them. The certificate can be useful for their future careers.

Using a certain promotion system is also a good motivation way. Those who prove a good leadership will be upgraded position.

Certainly, to success with lean, people should believe in the process and that they are doing the improving for their work to become easier, and safer not to get rewarded. They should be allowed to share and put their own ideas under a self-motivated and cooperative system to improve their own works. Also with a stable environment, the overall company's profitability will increase allowing more jobs for the labor force.

What to consider in a motivation system?

✓ Allow employee to share their own ideas for improving their own works. This will make the employee feel themselves and that they are valuable to the process. Employee should consider the improvement an enjoyable part of their work rather than a new method to follow. Giving people a degree of autonomy will increase the self-motivation.

✓ Use a certain system for promoting positions. Who will be promoted is who will prove good leadership and problem-solving capabilities. Leaders who failed to meet the challenge or achieve the targets won't be punished, but will have fewer people reporting to them and may go through more training cycles.

✓ Senior leaders should act as mentors for the younger leaders. And younger leaders should develop the working teams. Such a training system will make better environment for learning and encourage self-development. People should learn how to improve themselves continuously through practicing what they learn. In such a culture, the system will be appreciated by everyone. People learn more by doing, and then the practical improvement will increase their learning experience and meet the company's needs at the same time.

✓ People are most likely to make progress on goals that are broken into concrete, measurable actions, with some kind of structured accountability and positive reinforcement.

✓ Avoid incentives that are based on individual accomplishments and use awards for team accomplishments and plant performance. Japan's culture believes that there is no reason to incentivize exceptional performance when it is what is expected, however, with the other different cultures like America, Europe, Africa, there is a use of some rewards and a bonus system that is based on a group performance.

The Do Phase

O ver the past few years, companies were striving to remove their wastes, adapting their processes and achieving operation excellence through lean methodology by hiring those lean experts who may promise to achieve the results and the cost reduction goals in short periods by implementing good plans!

Hiring the Lean Team-Who Is Responsible for Making Improvement?

Mistakenly, many companies tend to bring those outsourcing consultants to improve their processes and don't pay attention to training and coaching their regular employee. As if they are planning to relay on outsourcing forever! The consultants sometimes go ahead and hire some external lean experts and black belts six sigma holders to quickly improve the processes and achieve rapid results.

The company will create a continuous improvement department and relegate the development and the improvement behavior to this department. Such a parallel team will be powerless to effect change and make the improvement. They have lack of experience about the company's culture and lack of knowledge about the situation at the processes. They haven't been at the gemba before. Also, they are not responsible directly for the operations.

What usually happens when the outsourcing consultant leaves that all knowledge is gone. The regular employees will have no experience to keep managing the improved processes or continuously improving them to face the future challenges. They have not been trained on the culture of continuous improvement and have not been contributed in the transformation process. A part from the fact, that all powerful lean tools should be used by the company's leaders and the factory managers who have the capability, power, responsibility to effect changes.

Another issue appears from hiring those external lean experts and assigns the improvement efforts to them, the regular employee will treat the new hired team like a mistake hunter. People often see the metrics and other tools as poor examples of their performance and not as an opportunity to fix. This usually happens when metrics are used by an external team to control or evaluate the process rather than being a tool at the hand of the employee themselves to measure their own progress and define the requirements for the next step. For this reason, the regular employee might not cooperate with the new team. Worse, trying to damage their work and act as road blockers in the improvement process. This working environment has a very negative effect on the company's success.

If a company was to establish a professional group or team, the initial purpose of this team should be developing familiarity with these lean tools and how they work. They know more about how each tool is working. The group will be responsible for mentoring, coaching, and developing the leader's capabilities. Also monitoring, adjusting, and developing the continuous improvement culture of the organization. This group may need an external adviser/coacher as well, but the group won't be responsible directly for the process improvement, or all mentoring processes at the operation levels. That will be the responsibility of the managers and leaders at each level and in each area in the organization.

At Toyota, the responsibility of the daily kaizen is led by those who are responsible for operations not by a continuous improvement department or some outsourcing consultants. The leaders who manage the work day by day will be responsible for coaching people who do the work. And together those people will own, operate, develop, and continually improve their processes.

The Check Phase

There is no reason to say that companies should not try to get rapid results with the implementation of lean in everywhere in the company and at every process. But this should be done without scarifying the learning. Culture adaptiveness and leaders' development are very important in order to get sustainable results, otherwise, the improvement will be a short-lived one. All efforts, resources, and tools that have been spent to achieve the results will be lost.

Aligning the Improvement Efforts with The Overall Demanded Outcomes for Maximum Efficiency

You should check if the improvement made is aligned with the goals and the strategic plans and not creating problems in other areas, then re plan and re do in the "act" phase.

Lots of companies tend to focus on improving as many individual processes as possible using a tool like VSM rather than focusing on the whole value stream. In the value stream you look at a series of processes together. This gives better results and ensures the quality of improvement.

The focus on maximizing the efficiency and the capability of a single process can negatively affect another process. Processes shouldn't be improved at the expense of the others.

For example, one of the main lean goals is to make one piece flow through the production processes and minimize the work in process WIP inventory. If you are assembling one piece of product in 10 minutes, the wait to assemble 10 pieces and send them together in one large batch is 100 minutes, so the time of assembling one piece has become 100 minutes although the value-added time is only 10 minutes. Moving one piece of product every 10 minutes will reduce the lead times of making the product, minimize the WIP inventory and speed up the delivery to the customer. But this can put load on the transportation process and increase the efforts especially when the process steps are not close to each other's. So, improving the efficiency of the transportation process should be also considered. Producing with small batches may be a good compromise. And to continuously improve this process and provide one piece of product or reduce the batches size, you have to continuously improve the transportation too and eliminate all obstacles.

Although analyzing the whole value stream usually give good results over the analysis of the individual processes, but analyzing the individual processes and improving them can give quicker result. Usually, when analyzing a series of processes in the value stream there will be also a series of issues that are linked together. They will take much longer time to be improved and may need to be divided into small issues and each will go through the continuous improvement cycle P-D-C-A. This is not usually works when there are many companies out there that still don't believe about the workability of lean. In such a culture it is preferably to show quick results by looking at the processes that can be improved easily and quickly and avoid waiting to improve the overall value stream that will take longer time to fix. When the top management sees quick results from lean, they will provide the support needed for more improvement.

Value stream mapping VSM is a good lean tool that is being used to improve the process. A part from the fact that VSM is not exactly a tool for process improvement rather than a tool to insure that process improvement efforts:

✓ Fit together from a process to process so that a flowing value stream is developed.

✓ Match with the organization's targets and business needs.

✓ Serve the requirements of the external customers.

Some companies utilize the VSM to make improvement as found and perform random improvement for discovered wastes without having a clear vision that based on the current situation and the real business needs. It is better to perform VSM based on reasonable objectives and specific plans in order to reflect the change and improve the overall company's business process.

Tips

The Use of Cost Benefit Analysis in Decision Making

F requently, cost benefit analysis is being carried by those accountants and inexperienced estimators to determine the beneficial of the next step required in the lean improvement initiative during the plan phase.

For example, a common mistake made by many manufacturing is the arrangement of the machines by similarity rather than by the sequence of the process steps. This system hides many wastes behind it. The transportation cost will be increased allowing more resources to be used to transfer one piece of product from a process to another. There will be much WIP inventory buildup between the process steps and a process might have to wait until it gets the material it needs for work. This will affect the external customers, delay the product delivery, and affect the quality too.

Indeed, machines arrangement should take into consideration the following things: minimizing the WIP inventory, minimizing the time it takes to produce one piece of product, be faster than the takt time which is the customer demand rate for a product or group of products. And consider all workstations, machines, and operation tools to be as close as possible to avoid waiting for tools or parts issue and what is called ergonomics in the workplace.

Commonly, when a cost benefit analysis CBA is performed, the cost of re arranging the machines would be very high on the short-terms. But the main lean goal is to make one piece flow, minimize the WIP inventory, and shorten the lead times which have proven to give remarkable results on the long-terms. So, the CBA if considered over months, years, the cost of doing the job once and for all will be less than the cost of keeping the situation as it is with all the wastes. Also, customer satisfaction and delivery speeds should be considered as customer are what keep any organization in business.

At this case, CBA can be carried to determine the best method that should be used to re arrange the machines not to decide whether to make it or not. Also, the CBA can be useful to determine the speed of making the changeover.

Short-term Focus on Cost Reduction

The traditional working environment often presents a lack of trustiness between the labors who are working at the down operation level and the managers who are working at the top management level. There is always a resistant between both. Managers treat labors like machines, over burden them to achieve the company's goals. The rule is: "extract the maximum for lowest fees." And labors try to preserve their jobs and use some tricks to keep working with their preferable method constraining any improvement.

Worse, if lean is being used as a resource's reduction tool, no real improvement will be gained. As long as labors believe that lean and other improvement methods will make them lose their jobs, they will not buy-in. Apart from the fact that the lean savings would be meaningless in terms of savings when a company have a large excess in capacity, if a company decide then to lay off the people, all of the savings will be blamed on lean.

In a company that was driving a bad culture and remove labors after each improvement project. The labors have been heard saying: "last time we did this improvement half of us lost their jobs, we have to keep working as we are to preserve our jobs."

An industrial engineer at the same company was measuring the time it takes to complete a specific process using a stop watch and counting the time of each work step in order to develop a work standard procedure. Labors were noted using some tricks to expand the time it takes to complete each part of the work, making the lean job harder.

When a company decide to start the improvement process by eliminating wasted motions on the shop floor; this will lead to removal of workers from a line or cell, those workers should be placed on another job so less workers have to be hired in the future. What Toyota production system does it provides something to do with any extra regular employees; such as work in kaizen teams to improve on standardized work, improve downtimes, identify the root causes of quality problems and develop countermeasures, train more deeply in problem solving, and find better ways to move materials.

Generally, companies that want to build a good lean culture should avoid connecting the kaizen work to the layoff process. Some companies have realized this, so they tend to transfer the extra labor from one line to another or use them in elsewhere in the company to avoid the layoff.

To maintain good relation and a foundation of trust between the top management and the workers, a few gemba walks can be considered by managers that should include: watching the working environment to grasp if something is wrong that could affect the safety at the working area, monitor to see if operators are performing any unsafe act, monitor the working environment for further problems that are preventing labors from doing their jobs smoothly such as no tools available in place, no spare parts, delay in transportation of material, and the existence of unsafe equipment in the working area like forklifts, and give high priority and commitment to the workplace cleaning and organization (like doing 5S). With such a clean, safe, and comfortable environment, labors will feel that everyone in the company is committed to the employee safety and satisfaction as well as the improvement, and development of the working process to make things easier and not just the targets and accomplishments.

Workers must be treated like appreciated assets, and because process is being continuously improved by those who are involved directly in the operations under the leadership of the operation managers, so the value of those workers will be increasing time by time.

There are many lessons to learn from Japan Toyota. Liker and Convis (2012) expressed that Toyota responded to the crises of recalls and recession by doing more kaizen, and more self-development, and used the opportunity to build a more stable foundation for the future. Toyota didn't close any of its plants and didn't lay off the regular employee. Unfortunately, we see companies in the recession time's cut-costs and reduce wages and their first thinking would jump into pause any training process in order to reduce the overheads.

However, in crisis situations, some companies are forced to sell assets or layoff people in order to survive and avoid bankruptcy. What is mentioned is the culture that should be maintained in almost stable environments. Layoff should not be an easy tool and a normal habit for cost reduction. It has a very negative effect on companies that want to maintain a good culture and gain sustainability with lean. Actually, some companies have a very reactive culture and short-term focused. When the sales are down, they immediately put pressure on people to make them leaves in order to cut costs and keep the profitability at the same level. 40

What Is Behind Success?

People must have degree of security and feel they belong to the team. Jobs must be designed to be challenging. People need some autonomy to feel they have control over the job. Nothing motivating as challenging the targets, constant measurement, and feedback on progress, and an occasional reward based on group accomplishments.

Although Toyota use its own business practice in defining strategies and goals, but there is no magical tool behind the Toyota success. Liker (2012) summarized six points to be made for any organization that wants to begin the continuous improvement journey:

1.There must be a shared vision that is believable actionable and reinforced in concrete terms as the work is done.

2. Developing leaders that are willing to take the challenge through self-develop, and keep coaching them at the gemba.

3. Turn the role of leaders from decision makers to teachers so they can develop the other leaders.

4. Developing a continuous improvement culture through the plan-do-check-act to continuously improve the processes. Spend enough time at the plan and check phases, and avoid rapid jump to act phase.

5. Aligning the targets and plans to achieve the results and use problems solving to remove the obstacles.

6. Using the major challenges from the environment to further strengthen the company and the leaders to work toward a long-term vision like the respond of Toyota to the crises of recall, recession and Japan earthquakes.

Toyota uses a very deep and patient process to develop their internal leaders. Even most of trainings are being carried at the gemba, and very few are carried in classrooms. The formal classroom training is ineffective alone for changing people behaviors. The process was expressed deeply by Rother (2009).

It has been verified that to build exceptional people and teams, this must derive from having in place some form of a "respect for humanity system."

Appendix. I

Gemba

Gemba is a Japanese word meaning the actual place where value-creating work happens. Many leaders use gemba only for solving problems, visiting only when there is an issue. Others practice gemba walks on a daily basis to follow up and monitor the situation. However, Toyota believes that leaders truly develop through daily experiences at the gemba. In reality, gemba is a principle for managing, developing and improving people and processes. It is a valuable tool that helps lean practitioners learn the true facts so they can base management decisions on the actual situation.

In his book Managing to Learn, John Shook described the gemba as any setting in which individuals are creating value for the customer. This description goes beyond the manufacturing shop floor, which is how most lean practitioners describe the term. By going to the place where work is done, leaders gain firsthand, personal knowledge so they can understand the real situation and what needs to be fixed. Processes cannot be analyzed or understood from offices. Managing performance data from a distance carries huge negatives for leaders, as it could hide the reality of the situation. Leaders who have been at the gemba can make decisions and take responsibility of problem-solving.

Many organizations are developing a standard for their leaders that includes checklists for what should be observed during the gemba walk. More important for every department is to create value for the customer at the gemba by eliminating the non-value-added work that increases the product price, reduces quality and delays delivery.

Gemba and Solving Problems

Don't rush the solution! Take the example of a fertilizer company that face machine downtime problems. The issue, which involved a poorly performing centrifugal fan, reduced production availability by 20 percent. The fan vibrated a lot and suffered balancing issues. Shutting down the fan for balancing four times in a month cost thousands of dollars in production losses and maintenance costs.

Everyone in the factory believed that this was a direct maintenance problem related to machine balancing, so maintenance should design a solution. Instead of moving forward with that solution, a kaizen team was assigned to observe the situation. After two days at the gemba analyzing the process, the team concluded that the problem was a process design issue. And of the two process issues causing the problem, neither was the fan. The fertilizer company needed to fix the process to eliminate the downtime instead of concentrating on the fan, which kept the issue at the problem-fix cycle. Without real observation at the gemba, the kaizen team could not have realized the true issue.

This example reveals how many problems are hidden and cannot be discovered from reading the performance data. If a machine is waiting for loading, the problem could include having no orders to process, transportation issues, a work-in-process inventory issue or all of the above. Downtime could have associated activities such as searching for tools, searching for spare parts, waiting for operators and other issues. In any case, production wastes need to be eliminated to reduce lead-times and meet the customer takt time (the customer demand rate). Employees who do the work each day should be taught how to surface these issues in a visual board so leaders can see them and support improvements.

The basic steps of any problem-solving process through the plan-do-check-act (PDCA) cycle are:

1. Define the problem relative to the ideal (plan).

2. Break down the problem into manageable pieces (plan).

3. Find the root cause of the problem (plan).

4. Set the targets for achievement (plan).

5. Select the suitable solution from different countermeasures (plan).

6. Implement the plan (do).

7. Revise the outcomes as expected (check).

8. Find out what is going wrong, adapt, adjust, and then repeat the cycle (act).

As you can see, the plan phase is invoked five times before proceeding to the do phase. This is to ensure both the quality of the implementation and that the selected countermeasure will solve the problem. The plan phase cannot be created without a daily observation at the gemba. And finding the root cause of any issue requires a deep observation at the gemba, gathering facts, discussing things with the process operators and developing the best countermeasure from different alternatives.

Unfortunately, many leaders would jump into the do phase without spending enough time observing the situation to find the root cause. The most enjoyable part for the leader is the "do," but jumping to the do means not enough time has been spent on understanding. A quick fix not only might not solve the real problem, it could create wastes in other linked areas.

Lean decision-making assessing a set of potential countermeasures rather than just one approach. This minimizes risk and allows people who do the work to discuss different ideas from a wide range of potential scenarios to implement the best solution, a fix that will solve the issue without creating other problems or wastes. Often, those countermeasures are first developed and taken from different people at the gemba.

After selecting and testing the countermeasures, the continuous improvement leader should draw a Gantt chart and define target deadlines based on the recommendation of people who do the work. Define the rest of the activities, such as who will do the plan, how they will develop the plan, and when and how the work will be done. Finally, assign responsibilities for each deliverable and confirm targets and dates.

In recent decades, the quality issue often has been tackled via Six Sigma improvement initiatives. Six Sigma collects data and runs it through statistical component-correlation, regression and analysis for variation. Even though some output results are statistically significant, in many cases Six Sigma teams don't truly understand what is going on?

At Toyota, rather than immediately turning to complex statistical tools, the genchi genbustu process (gemba) also mean "go and see where the work is done" and other simple analysis tools are tackling the issue of quality. With quality problems, the intention from the gemba visit should be revising the work against the standard, monitoring the operator's work, understanding the reasons by asking the "five whys," benchmarking the process with others, reviewing the standard process chart and updating it accordingly to prevent the error in the future.

Read one of my best-selling books *"Gemba Walks the Toyota Way"*

Appendix. II

Toyota Coaching Process

Toyota believes that employees can learn more by doing, by understanding the situation through grasping the reality of the gemba. Ideally, this means teaching on the shop floor, in the office, or at the shipping dock rather than at a formal training meeting. At Toyota, the process of fixing problems is used to teach a new way of thinking.

At Toyota, every leader takes the responsibility of developing another leader. Leaders who know how the process works at the gemba coach their mentees on problem-solving and process improvement methods. The rule is that leaders cannot teach what they cannot do. In Japan, they don't teach management in classrooms, as most learning happens at the gemba. As presented by Jeffrey K. Liker in his book The Toyota Way to Lean Leadership, the learning process at Toyota is called shu ha ri, three terms that refer to three stages of learning.

Shu means to protect. In this phase, students are coached on the fundamentals under the watchable eye of the master. Ha means to break away. In this phase, the student has more freedom to practice unsupervised. The master may check on her; the student can apply the rules creatively but will follow the standard rigidly.

Ri means freedom, and in this phase, rules and behaviors have become so ingrained that the student no longer thinks about them consciously. These students are now in the position to develop their own understanding.

Think about the work standard. A worker first must learn how to assemble parts onsite by following the standard work procedures. He will learn by doing. In the shu stage, he will see how the work is done and try to follow the teacher. The worker will practice the job continuously until he reaches the second step, ha. The teacher will keep monitoring him until he reaches the final stage, ri. At this stage, the worker can observe the overall working procedures and take the responsibility to improve them.

By coaching and mentoring people on processes at the gemba and using real problems to improve leadership skills, Toyota's employees and managers become more professional at solving issues in the future while developing other leaders. Mike Rother presents a great example in his Toyota Kata book. In chapter eight, the mentor used a real quality problem in the assembly line to improve the skills of the mentee. Although the mentor figured out the solution quickly, he never told the mentee. Instead, the mentor allowed the mentee a degree of freedom to think and develop his own ideas to solve the problem. This shows how to transfer the mentee from the ha phase to the ri phase.

Appendix. III

Lean Resources

There are many books and articles written on lean leadership and management that this book cites. They are all listed at the end of the book and I also include additional recommended resources for further reading:

Borris, S. 2012. *Strategic Lean Mapping*. New York: McGraw-Hill.

Harris, R., C. Harris, and Earl Wilson. 2003. *Making Materials Flow: A Lean Material Handling Guide for Operations, Production-Control, and Engineering Professionals*. Cambridge, MA: Lean Enterprise Institute.

Liker, J. K., and K. J. Franz. 2011. *The Toyota Way to Continuous Improvement: Linking Strategy and Operational Excellence to Achieve Superior Performance*. New York: McGraw-Hill.

Rother, M., and R. Harris. 2001. *Creating Continuous Flow: An Action Guide for Managers, Engineers and Production Associates*. Cambridge, MA: Lean Enterprise Institute.

Shook, J. 2008. *Managing to Learn: Using the A3 Management Process to Solve Problems, Gain Agreement, Mentor and Lead*. Cambridge, MA: Lean Enterprise Institute.

Soliman, M. H. A. 2014. *The Seven Deadly Wastes and How to Remove Them from Your Business: The Heart of the Toyota Production System*. Personal-lean.org.

Rother, M. (2009). *Toyota Kata: Managing People for Improvement, Adaptiveness, And Superior Results*. New York: Macgraw-Hill.

REFERENCES

Shook. J. (2008). Managing to Learn: Using the A3 Management Process to Solve Problems, Gain Agreement, Mentor and Lead. Cambridge, MA: Lean Enterprise Institute.

Drucker, P. F. (1954). The Practice of Management. New York: HarperCollins Publishers.

Taylor, F. W. (1911). The Principles of Scientific Management. New York: Harper & Brothers.

Liker, J. K., & Convis, G. L. (2012). Toyota Way to Lean Leadership: Achieving and Sustaining Excellence Through Leadership Development. New York: Macgraw-Hill.

Rother, M. (2009). Toyota Kata: Managing People for Improvement, Adaptiveness, And Superior Results. New York: Macgraw-Hill.

Ahmed, M. H. (2013). Lean Transformation Guidance: Why Organizations Fail to Achieve and Sustain Excellence through Lean Improvement. International Journal of Lean Thinking 4 (1): 31–40.

Ahmed, M. H. (2014). Daily Walks Train Future Leaders. Industrial Management 56 (1): 22–27.

Soliman, M. H. A. 2015. A New Routine for Culture Change. Industrial Management 57 (3): 25–30.

Soliman, M. H. A. (2016). Developing People Improves the Process. Industrial Management 58 (1).

Soliman, M. H. A. (2014). Analyzing Failure to Prevent Problems. Industrial Management 56 (5): 10.

Soliman, M. H. A. (2016). Hoshin Kanri: How Toyota Creates a Culture of Continuous Improvement to Achieve Lean Goals. CreateSpace, South Carolina.

Soliman, M. H. A. (2020). Gemba Walks the Toyota Way: The Place to Teach and Learn Management. Personal-lean.org.

Liker, J. K., and G. L. Convis. 2012. The Toyota Way to Lean Leadership: Achieving and Sustaining Excellence through Leadership Development. New York: McGraw-Hill.

Liker, J. K., and G. Trachilis. 2015. Developing Lean Leaders at All Levels: A Practical Guide. Cambridge, MA: Lean Leadership Institute Publications.

Also, by Soliman

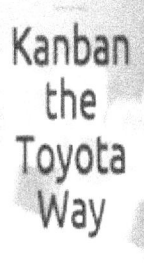

Don't miss out!

Visit the website below and you can sign up to receive emails whenever Mohammed Hamed Ahmed Soliman publishes a new book. There's no charge and no obligation.

https://books2read.com/r/B-A-VCQM-WFSBC

BOOKS 2 READ

Connecting independent readers to independent writers.

Did you love *Turning PDCA into a Routine for Learning*? Then you should read *Gemba Walks the Toyota Way : The Place to Teach and Learn Management*[1] by Mohammed Hamed Ahmed Soliman!

Gemba is a Japanese word meaning the actual place where value-creating work happens. Many leaders use gemba only for solving problems, visiting only when there is an issue. Others practice gemba walks on a daily basis to follow up and monitor the situation. However, Toyota believes that leaders truly develop through daily experiences at the gemba. In reality, gemba is a principle for managing, developing and improving

1. https://books2read.com/u/bpyWaX

2. https://books2read.com/u/bpyWaX

people and processes. It is a valuable tool that helps lean practitioners learn the true facts so they can base management decisions on the actual situation.

Read more at https://www.personal-lean.org/.

Also by Mohammed Hamed Ahmed Soliman

Hoshin Kanri: How Toyota Creates a Culture of Continuous Improvement to Achieve Lean Goals
The Seven Deadly Wastes and How to Remove Them from Your Business: The Heart of the Toyota Production System
Overall Equipment Effectiveness Simplified: Analyzing OEE to find the Improvement Opportunities
Machinery Oil Analysis & Condition Monitoring : A Practical Guide to Sampling and Analyzing Oil to Improve Equipment Reliability
Practical Guide to FMEA : A Proactive Approach to Failure Analysis
Industrial Applications of Infrared Thermography: How Infrared Analysis Can be Used to Improve Equipment Inspection
Ultrasound Analysis for Condition Monitoring: Applications of Ultrasound Detection for Various Industrial Equipment
Brainstorming for Problems Solving: How Leaders Can Achieve a Successful Brainstorming Session
Vibration Basics and Machine Reliability Simplified : A Practical Guide to Vibration Analysis

Gemba Walks the Toyota Way : The Place to Teach and Learn Management

Jidoka: The Toyota Principle of Building Quality into the Process

Lean Accounting : Why Accounting Department Should Switch to Lean

Turning PDCA into a Routine for Learning

Toyota Healthcare: 7+1 Types Of Waste

Kanban the Toyota Way: An Inventory Buffering System to Eliminate Inventory

Takt Time: A Guide to the Very Basic Lean Calculation

5S: A Practical Guide to Visualizing and Organizing Workplaces to Improve Productivity

Machine Reliability and Condition Monitoring: A Comprehensive Guide to Predictive Maintenance Planning

The Ultimate Guide to Successful Lean Transformation: Top Reasons Why Companies Fail to Achieve and Sustain Excellence through Lean Improvement

Toyota Standard Work: The Foundation of Kaizen

Risk Assessment Using FMEA: A Case of Reliable Improvement

5S: A Practical Guide to Visualizing and Organizing Workplaces to Improve Productivity

Hoshin Kanri: How Toyota Creates a Culture of Continuous Improvement to Achieve Lean Goals

Industrial Applications of Infrared Thermography: How Infrared Analysis Can be Used to Improve Equipment Inspection

Ultrasound Analysis for Condition Monitoring: Applications of Ultrasound Detection for Various Industrial Equipment

Watch for more at https://www.personal-lean.org/.

About the Author

Mohammed Hamed Ahmed Soliman is an industrial engineer, consultant, university lecturer, operational excellence leader, and author. He works as a lecturer at the American University in Cairo and as a consultant for several international industrial organizations. Soliman earned a bachelor of science in Engineering and a master's degree in Quality Management. He earned post-graduate degrees in Industrial Engineering and Engineering Management. He holds numerous certificates in management, industry, quality, and cost engineering. For most of his career, Soliman worked as a regular employee for various industrial sectors. This included crystal-glass making, fertilizers, and chemicals. He did this while educating people about the culture of continuous improvement. Soliman has lectured at Princess Noura University and trained the maintenance team in Vale Oman Pelletizing Company. He has been lecturing at

The American University in Cairo for 8 years and has designed and delivered 40 leadership and technical skills enhancement training modules. Soliman is a member at the Institute of Industrial and Systems Engineers and a member with the Society for Engineering and Management Systems. He has published several articles in peer reviewed academic journals and magazines. His writings on lean manufacturing, leadership, productivity, and business appear in Industrial Engineers, Lean Thinking, Industrial Management, and Sage Publications. Soliman's blog is www.personal-lean.org.

Read more at https://www.personal-lean.org/.

personal-lean.org

About the Publisher

Personal-lean is dedicated to publish high quality educational content, assessment, training in the filed of business for various industrial sectors. And is a growing educational organization, with products and services in various countries.